Who Will
Tell Your
Children
About
Jesus?

Who Will Tell Your Children About Jesus?

Alan Getts, M.D.

WINEPRESS **WP** PUBLISHING

Printed in South Korea.

Packaged by WinePress Publishing, PO Box 428, Enumclaw, WA 98022. The views expressed or implied in this work do not necessarily reflect those of WinePress Publishing. The author is ultimately responsible for the design, content, and editorial accuracy of this work.

Scripture quotations marked NIV are taken from the Holy Bible, New International Version, Copyright © 1973, 1978, 1984 by the International Bible Society. Used by permission of Zondervan Publishing House. The "NIV" and "New International Version" trademarks are registered in the United States Patent and Trademark Office by International Bible Society.

Scripture quotations marked KJV are taken from the King James Version of the Bible.

ISBN 1-57921-408-8
Library of Congress Catalog Card Number: 2001094160

DEDICATION

Dedicated to my precious wife, Rebecca, and
my children James, Mickale and Mallory
for their patience and for their unending
abilities to teach me new truths
about our Lord, Jesus Christ.

ACKNOWLEDGMENTS ⑤

I am grateful to my friend and pastor, Dr. Gene Smith, for his kind and thoughtful words in the foreword of this book. Also, just as he does to my daily life, Pastor Smith has reviewed the text and assisted in the accuracy of its content and the appropriateness of its use of Scripture. We in his congregation are blessed by Pastor Gene's ability to prune, shape and equip us for the work of the Lord.

TABLE of CONTENTS ⑤

FOREWORD ⟳

In my sixteen years of ministry, I have not met a more selfless man than Dr. Alan Getts. Nor have I known a more able pediatrician. Dr. Getts is a dedicated Christian, a faithful husband, a loving father, and a loyal friend. He is deeply committed to serving God and helping parents whose children receive medical attention at his practice in Augusta, Georgia. This small book is a large treasure waiting to be discovered by dads and moms who want to help their children live rich, full and meaningful lives. It contains godly wisdom and practical insights that will inspire and energize any family to reach its full potential. If the truth in this book is applied, it will insulate your children from the ever-increasing darkness that has come upon the world. Every parent should read this book.

—Gene M. Smith
Senior Pastor
In Focus Church

I am a Christian pediatrician. Nearly every day I interact with thirty to fifty different families and, due to the nature of my profession, we discuss problems. In doing this for almost twenty years, I have observed how families approach problems, how parents teach their children to approach problems, and how families survive from day to day and from crisis to crisis. I am convinced by these observations that most families are not familiar with Jesus Christ and include neither Jesus nor the Bible (His book of instructions) as important parts of their problem-solving mechanisms.

I cannot say that I can determine whether a particular family is a Christian family or not based solely on their problem-solving techniques. I do not always find a way to ask about their faith during my time with them. Regardless of what their answer may be, it is clear that most families are not trusting in Jesus Christ to help them in troubled times, nor are they teaching their children to do the same. That is why this book exists.

In preparing this book I start with certain assumptions:

I assume that God gave me this purpose.

The desire to prepare this book churned in me for two years before I began writing. During those years I saw many families confront crises without turning to Jesus. Each time, the Lord reminded me that godly encouragement and instruction for young parents is desperately needed. Each dilemma saddened me and then God prompted me anew to get started. Gradually He gave me the ideas and the outline. At last, I am getting on with the job. I know God is with me.

I assume that those who read this book fall into one of four categories.

First, some readers are Christian parents desiring to raise Christian children. (Let's define "Christian children" as children raised and instructed to know about Jesus Christ, to read and believe His Word, the Holy Bible, and to have a personal relationship with Jesus which is fostered by prayer, worship and regular involvement in a church body of other believers.)

Second, some readers are *friends or relatives of young parents* who want to assist these parents in the proper rearing of their children.

Third, many *parents, or parents-to-be*, are reading this book. These folks may have received this book as a gift.

Fourth and finally, some readers, probably Christians, are *just curious* about the topic.

To the friends, relatives and the curious, I thank you for your interest and I pray that you will find some blessing in the reading and be able to pass the same on to others. However, let me clearly state that this book is strictly aimed at the parents among you. Parents, this book is for you.

I assume that the parents reading this book desire to raise Christian children.

If you are a parent and this does not describe you, there is really no reason to read on since the entire body of this book is dedicated to that end.

I assume that most parents who read the rest of this book are already Christians and have a personal relationship with the Lord Jesus Christ.

Note that I said most parents. Some readers may not yet be Christians themselves, so let's make some things clear before we go any further.

Raising Christian children will be almost impossible if one or both parents do not know and believe in Jesus Christ. Surely, some children become Christians after growing up in non-Christian homes. But, by definition, these children were not "raised as Christians." Someone, somewhere, led or drew these children to Christ. It was not the parents' doing. *Such children exemplify the reason for this book.* Many children—too many children—do not learn about Jesus at home. The most influential people in children's lives, their parents, often bypass this great and honorable duty. I thank God that others do fill the gaps for some, but the truth remains that the best teachers, the parent (or parents), should teach their own children about Jesus and about Christian living. A non-Christian parent is just not up to this task.

Of course, besides wanting the best for your children, I am also greatly concerned for the eternity of any non-Christian parent. To die without knowing Jesus is Christ is the beginning of an eternity of isolation and pain. I pray that no one who has the chance to choose knowing Jesus and spending eternity with Him will make the choice of an eternity without Him.

So if you—yes, you, the reader—were not a Christian when you woke up this morning, I urge you to become one now and to spend your first night in God's family tonight! To these special readers I say: STOP RIGHT NOW! Don't go past this paragraph until you believe that Jesus is real. Believe that He is alive. Even though He died to pay the price for all of our wrongdoings, He rose from the dead and is alive. Believe that He loves you so much that He rejoices when you believe in Him.

To become a Christian, say this prayer to Jesus:

Jesus,
I believe You. You are the almighty God and You love me. I have done wrong things in my life and I deserve punishment, but I believe You when You say that You took my punishment for me. Lord, please live in me and direct my words and direct my steps as I, starting now, am a newborn Christian.

Thank You, Jesus.
Amen.

For the readers praying this prayer for the first time, I welcome you into the family of God. I am unspeakably excited about your decision! There is more to learn about being a Christian, and if you would be kind enough to write to me, I will send you some information that will help you get started. Contact me at either the regular mail or email address below. Please be sure to include a return address.

Dr. Alan Getts
PO Box 1758
Evans, Georgia 30809
agetts@pedpartners.com

With this important business completed, let's move on to the purpose of this book. It is my hope and desire to motivate and, when necessary, instruct parents in teaching their children about Jesus Christ. I am convinced that it is God's plan for all children to be instructed

> Kings of the earth, and all people; princes, and all judges of the earth: Both young men, and maidens; old men, and children: Let them praise the name of the Lord: for his name alone is excellent; his glory is above the earth and heaven.
>
> Psalm 148:11–13, KJV

about Jesus. (See Psalm 148:11–13.) I am likewise convinced that God's directions state that parents are to perform this duty. (See Proverbs 1:8–9.) Who else could do this? Who else is admired so much by children, and who else is present so often to continually teach and reinforce what has been taught before?

There are many forces in our society that neglect or outright obstruct the teaching of Christ to children. Such forces have been widely successful which is why teaching about Jesus is often just not done. In many other

> Listen, my son, to your father's instruction and do not forsake your mother's teaching. They will be a garland to grace your head and a chain to adorn your neck.
>
> Proverbs 1:8–9, NIV

circumstances, even when teaching about Jesus does happen, it is presented in such a meaningless or halfhearted manner that the lessons are quickly forgotten or are never taken to heart in the first place.

That is why this book is in your hands: To encourage you, to prompt you, to help you tell your children about Jesus Christ. And not simply to relay information, but to tell them in ways that are remembered and believed forever, change their lives forever, and place your children in the kingdom of God.

CHAPTER ONE 🌀

Who Will Tell Your Children About Jesus Christ?

I have a sister-in-law named Mary who lives far away, so my family rarely gets to see her. Mary is an adult about my age. She lives in her own apartment and has a small job. She depends on her parents and the staff at her residence to protect her and assist her with her daily tasks because Mary is mentally retarded.

Every holiday, without fail, Mary sends a very nice greeting card to our family, as well as to others, I'm sure. My wife and I read the cards, politely write back, including the latest photo of our children or the entire family in the envelope. We rarely share the cards with our children. Mary's handwriting is hard to read and, from our perspective, she doesn't write very much. Of course, the children are welcome to read the cards, but we usually put the cards on our dresser until it's time to put them away.

Months—maybe even years—often go by in which we never speak Mary's name in our house. My wife and I think of her often, but we don't discuss her much. Consequently our children know very little about her.

One summer my youngest daughter, then 16, and I went to visit my in-laws—her grandparents and Mary's parents—and Mary. After dinner and chatting with her grandparents and Mary, my daughter asked me questions about Mary. Why was she different? Where did she live? How did she get by each day? Why was she mentally retarded?

I was embarrassed to acknowledge that I had never told my children much about Mary. My wife's precious only sister just was not a big part of our lives. We love her and we care about how she's doing, but we have never told our children—her nieces and nephew—very much about her.

Later, when I took the time to tell all of our children more about Mary, my earlier error became clear. I hadn't realized that they *really* wanted to know more about their aunt. I finally understood that things I find important—things that are close to me—*are* important to my children. The simple fact that things or people matter to parents also causes those things and people to matter to their children. That's God's plan, I guess. There seems to be nothing we can do to change it. Perhaps this phenomenon is part of what we call our heritage.

Most families treat Jesus just like we treat my sister-in-law. If we know Jesus, we love Him.

And we care for Him, but He just isn't a part of our lives that we discuss. Months and years can go by without ever saying His name in our homes, and our children never seem to learn about Him.

I fear that if we parents don't mention Jesus often enough, someone else in our children's lives will. Probably that someone will be a person or character on *television*. Since the average child spends over thirty hours per week watching television, somewhere in those hundreds of hours they're sure to learn about Jesus. But will it be correct information?

That's highly unlikely. The content of today's television sitcoms, talk shows, cartoons, sports broadcasts, and even commercials is far from god-like. It is more likely that television will teach children how OK it is to drink alcoholic beverages, how sexy it is to dress provocatively, or how "normal" a person can be while pursuing a deviant lifestyle. But they will not learn about

Jesus—at least not the right information—on television.

Admittedly there are uncommon programs, usually not on the main networks, that portray Jesus and Christianity in positive terms. Most main-stream programming, however, criticizes God, Jesus and Christians. It paints the picture that only people who are weak or stupid believe in Jesus Christ. One prominent network owner went so far as to say: "Christianity is for losers."

You get the picture. Your children will not learn the truth about Jesus Christ while they watch today's popular television programming.

What about Christian television stations?

Well now, these may be a good start. Of course, to learn from these stations your children will actually have to be tuned in and watching the programs. Can you name the Christian channels on your television? How many hours per week are these channels playing in your home? Are your children watching?

If your children do watch Christian programming, who is it that helps them understand the messages and apply them to their own lives? If they watch and you don't watch with them, what lesson have you taught them regarding how much you value the teaching that is broadcast? Let's be honest. While Christian television stations can teach your children some things about Jesus, we do not watch enough, nor do we discuss the programs enough or reinforce the teachings enough for this source to accurately teach your children about Jesus.

What about Christian radio?

This is another option, but the same questions apply. Do you know the frequencies of the Christian radio stations in your area? Do your children ever listen to them? Do you ever tune in? When your children jump into your car and turn on the radio, what station do they hear that you listen to? Once again, this medium just isn't enough to teach your children about Jesus. In fact, if most of your children's radio and CD listening is to non-Christian music, they will likely hear so much anti-Christian content that any impact made by the Christian stations will be washed away.

Well, what about at school?

Don't kids teach each other about Jesus? Wouldn't it be great if some of the six to eight hours of each school day were spent learning about Jesus, the God who created the earth (and the schoolhouse)? Oh, wait now: reality check! Remember that in 1963 our government removed God from public schools. Since then, God's enemies have succeeded in removing Bibles, Christian instruction, the Ten Commandments, and classroom prayer as well. Where can Jesus be discussed in school now?

I am greatly concerned that today's new parents never had the privilege of praying or discussing Jesus in school. In fact, it is highly likely that a school-age child today does not have a parent or any teacher who remembers what it was like to pray and talk about Jesus while in the schoolhouse! Most children have no role models that remember "how it used to be." And with the current school environment so paranoid about God it has become hostile to Him, there are very few chances that your children will ever have any meaningful discussion about Jesus at school, on the playground, in the classroom, or with anyone else attending their school. So much for school being a resource.

Can you count on your children's friends to teach your kids about Jesus?

I pray for you and your children that your kids will find friends who know Jesus, who will share with your children about Him. Truthfully, however, how likely is that? With our current social focus on brand-name clothes, sports and sports figures, pop music, boyfriends and girl-friends, do you think Jesus has a chance of coming up in youngsters' conversations?

Can even Christian children, who make up less than one-half of all children, be bold enough to repeatedly risk humiliation by discussing Christ with their friends, your children? Peer pressure is an ominous force. And thanks to the movies, music, and politics of our time, even if your child doesn't try to embarrass an outspoken young Christian, somebody else's child most likely will. "Jesus talk" has thus been successfully muted in our children's public conversations. Your children will not learn about Jesus among the majority of their friends.

Well, there's always Sunday school to teach children about Jesus.

Yes! I hope your children are in Sunday school regularly. I expect that your children will be told about Jesus in Sunday school, and I applaud you if you regularly keep your children in a Sunday school class.

There are some concerns, however, that I ask you to consider before putting all your eggs into the Sunday school basket:

First, can a Sunday school teacher teach about Jesus better than you can? Can one hour on Sunday morning be remembered for an entire week until the next lesson? Can one hour of teaching and encouragement undo all the confusion or harm caused by listening to what television, radio, or friends say about Jesus?

I am convinced that one hour of teaching a week is not enough time to give your children all the information they need about Jesus. Parents, however, can make this one-hour lesson "last all week" by doing some simple reinforcement Monday through Saturday. For example, after class you can ask about the weekly lesson and expand on it, exploring together ways to use the truths that were taught. Make up scenarios or ask questions that demonstrate how to apply the lesson to daily events.

Simply rereading the lesson *with* your children will do great things in reemphasizing important points and, best of all, will demonstrate that *you care enough* about the lessons to read them, too. Likewise, when parents attend a similar class for adults they underscore the importance they place on Sunday school for the entire family. These parents' children will then take their own class more seriously. (Remember what we said about "heritage"?)

Sunday school lessons can also be reinforced any day of the week. When a situation arises that relates to the class subject, take time to remind your children what they learned. Help them put in place and actually live up to the standards they study at church. Most important of all, when *you live up to the standards* your children have just been taught, *you* demonstrate the importance of Sunday school and you give *living* lessons as you "practice what you preach."

Well, it seems we have brought this matter right back to you, the parent(s). I am sure that by now you have deduced that it is *your* duty, *your* honor, and *your* pleasure to be the one(s) who tell your children about Jesus. To borrow a line from an old Carly Simon song, "Nobody does it better." Nobody can teach your children as well as you can because you have the opportunity to demonstrate your teaching twenty-four hours a day, seven days a week. Also, nobody can *reach* your children as well as you can because what matters to you *will* matter to them. That is your children's heritage, and every child yearns to know and live out his heritage.

You are your children's primary teacher. What you say and, even more, what you do establish your children's morals and values for the rest of their lives. Let me say that again, WHAT YOU SAY AND, EVEN MORE, WHAT YOU DO ESTABLISH YOUR CHILDREN'S MORALS AND VALUES FOR THE REST OF THEIR LIVES.

Consider the following definitions from the *American Heritage Dictionary*:

> Morals: *Rules or habits of conduct . . . with reference to standards of right and wrong.*

> Values: *Principles, standards, or qualities considered worthwhile or desirable.*

Yes, as you teach your children, your behavior means even more than your words. You can reinforce and strengthen, or you can tear down and destroy, what your children learn at church by what you say and even more by what you do. For this reason, you actually have no choice.

You will tell your children about Jesus. Even if you don't use words to tell them about Jesus, you actually teach them many things. If you never mention Jesus, you teach them that you don't care about Him. If you never go to Sunday school or church or read your Bible or go over their Sunday school lessons with them, you teach them that you don't care to know anything about Jesus. And if you never let His name enter into your discussions or never pray to Him or never attend church, you teach them that Jesus is not important enough to take up any of your (or their) time.

So you do communicate to your children about Jesus in one way or another. You can *really* tell them and invest in the most important lesson and decision of their entire lives, or you can do nothing. If you do nothing, others will do your job for you. (But what kind of job will they do?) Or, to your shame, you may even interfere with others trying to teach the lessons that only you should be teaching them. In either of these last two scenarios, you treat Jesus just the same as I treated my sister-in-law, Mary.

CHAPTER TWO ⑤

What Will You Tell Your Children About Jesus?

Now that we clearly know it is you, the parent, who must tell your children about Jesus Christ, let's move on to discovering *what* you will tell them. To really understand who Jesus was while He was here on earth, it will be helpful (actually *mandatory*) to begin with a historical picture of Jesus, His life and His accomplishments. You will do better at accomplishing this if you have a Bible that you and your children can read and understand.

Depending on the ages of your children, adult Bibles may be overwhelming and may actually hinder their learning. Also, the language of some versions of the Bible will not be familiar to children and will interfere with their understanding. A Bible written for children will have simpler language and may have pictures that emphasize the key parts of the text. I know that I gained much new understanding when I read to my three-year-old from his Bible. I needed the basics and the pictures, too. Even beyond the historical Jesus, however, there will be much, much more you will need to tell your children. (More on that at the end of the chapter.)

The book of Matthew is my favorite part of the Bible for recounting the life of Jesus on earth. This is a great place to begin telling your children about Him. To assist you in telling them, here are some highlights from this first book of the New Testament.

For each key teaching point I have referenced the chapter and verse where you can find the corresponding Bible text. A reference written as (4:6) indicates that you can find that part of the story in the fourth chapter and the sixth verse. All chapters and verses can be found in the book of Matthew unless another book of the Bible is indicated. Here are some essential things your children need to know about Jesus' life on earth:

§ Jesus was born in Bethlehem by a miracle from God (1:18–2:1). I would save the discussion of Jesus' virgin birth for older children who might understand the concept more readily.

§ Jesus' birth and His life on earth were predicted by men who lived many years before Jesus was ever born (Isaiah 52:13–53:12).

§ Jesus is God (John 1:1–16).

§ The devil, Satan, tempted Jesus to sin but Jesus did not ever sin (4:3–11).

§ Jesus preached and taught all around the area of Judea and Galilee and brought hundreds of people into the family of God because He helped them understand that He was God's Son. He taught people what God really wanted them (and us) to be like (chapters 5, 6 and 7). It would be good to use a globe or world map to show your children where Jesus lived.

§ He performed many miracles like healing diseases and providing food for hungry people when there was no food. All of His miracles were done in order to help people and to demonstrate how much He loved all people (8:1–17; 14:15–21, 34–36, and several others). This was also one way to prove that He was the Son of God.

֍ He even brought dead people back to life when He knew that their families believed He was the Son of God (9:18–26; Luke 7:12–15).

֍ Jesus told people that He was the Son of God, but many did not believe it (16:13–17; Mark 2:1–12).

֍ The leaders of that time did not believe that Jesus was the Son of God. They decided to kill Jesus because He told the people that the leaders were corrupt (12:14).

֍ Jesus explained that the reason He had been sent to earth was to save the lost. That meant He was sent to teach people properly about God and to teach them how to live so that they could go to heaven with God. He taught that the only way for this to happen was for Him to be killed. After three days, He would rise and live again (16:1–12, 21; 20:17–19).

ෂ Jesus' most important lesson was that the way we can go to heaven is to believe that what He said was true and that He is the Son of God (John 3:16).

ෂ He taught there are two great commandments we should live by. If we do just these two, we will serve God well (22:36–39).

ෂ He taught that forgiving others is an important part of showing how we love others (6:14–15; Ephesians 4:32).

ෂ Jesus was betrayed by one of His closest friends and turned over to the authorities who put Him in jail (26:14–16, 47–56).

🔊 At a trial Jesus was found to be innocent, but the evil leaders persuaded the governor to kill Jesus anyway (27:20–24).

🔊 Jesus was killed; that is, His body died. But His spirit still lived and on the third day His body was raised to live and walk and talk again (28:1–10).

🔊 His death was necessary to satisfy God's laws. God requires a perfect (sinless) sacrifice to take away sin. Jesus died as *the* sacrifice for *our* sins. Because of Him all our sins for all time have been forgiven (Hebrews 9:12, 22).

🔊 Jesus later rose to heaven and is there with God for the purpose of being the future judge of all people—alive or dead—that come before Him (16:27; 26:64; Revelation 7:9–17; 20:11–15).

§ As He left earth he gave us an important command to spread the good news of His life and His promises to all people in the earth (28:18–20).

§ He promised that He will come again and rule the earth with great power (24:30–31; 26:64; John 14:28).

These high points of Jesus' life make a great beginning for teaching about Him. However, as I said earlier, knowing Jesus requires much more than just a history lesson. Points in history are easily forgotten, but lessons that affect the heart will last a lifetime.

Getting your children to really know Jesus will take more than teaching history. You will need to teach them *living* lessons from your heart—lessons that can be written permanently on their hearts. I encourage you to add these lessons from your own experience as you teach your children about Jesus.

Your own relationship with Jesus

Teach your children how, when and why you pray to Jesus. How did you come to know Jesus? What name do you call Him when you talk to him in prayer? What do you find is the best time to pray? What things do you talk to Him about? How do you ask God to forgive you? What do you say or do after you realize there is something He wants you to do? Do you pray with your eyes open, or with your eyes closed? (By the way, both are OK!)

Your examples of really speaking to and about Jesus make it clear to your children that you believe Jesus is real and that He is Lord. *Make your belief so real to them that it builds up their belief in Him as their Savior and Lord.* Pray out loud with your children. Remember that they learn more from what you do than from what you say. Actions do speak louder than words.

How you follow Jesus' commandments

Show your children what the great commandments mean to you. Let them see you put what Jesus said into practice every day of your life. (See Matthew 22:36–40.) Allow your children to hear and see how you follow Jesus' instructions, let-

> Master, which is the great commandment in the law? Jesus said unto him, Thou shalt love the Lord thy God with all thy heart, and with all thy soul, and with all thy mind. This is the first and great commandment. And the second is like unto it, Thou shalt love thy neighbour as thyself. On these two commandments hang all the law and the prophets.
>
> Matthew 22:36–40, KJV

ting them observe how highly you value what Jesus commanded. Doing so will bring his teachings to life in a way that your children can see and experience. Your teaching will mean so much more to your children when they see that you really "practice what you preach." After all, that is what creates the heritage your children need.

An important part of this lesson is also to teach your children what happens when we fail to keep Jesus' commandments. Teach them that Jesus knows we all sin; yet, He has already forgiven all our sins. Go back to the first point in this chapter and teach again about praying for forgiveness. Jesus will forgive us when we ask Him. What really matters is that we move on, trying our very best not to sin any more.

What being a Christian has done for you

We do not become Christians just to see what that experience can do for us, or for what we can get out of Christianity. (In fact, please don't think I recommend communicating such a message.) However, once you become a Christian, your life—like *every* new Christian's life—will change. Although your children probably aren't ready to be privy to any sordid details (if there are any in your life), tell your children how you have changed, how your life has changed, and what difference being a Christian has made in your life. Give examples of how you handle situations differently now compared to the way you handled them before you knew Jesus.

When your children hear what God has done and what blessings you have received, you are a *living* lesson to them, demonstrating that God's promises are true. This is a good time to remind your children of God's greatest promise: We can live in heaven with Him if we believe Him. If they are ready, lead them through the prayer in the introduction of this book!

You may feel that you don't have a lot to share from your life experiences in these particular areas yet. This is especially true for new Christians who may think they haven't been around God long enough to have anything worthwhile to say. Don't worry. You have a lot of teaching time still in front of you. As you continue to tell your children about Jesus, God will continue to teach you. Just keep on telling!

Let me end this chapter on what to tell your children about Jesus by prompting you to pray. Ask God for the right words to share with your family and your children. I don't presume to have all the right answers. Far from it! I have only what the Lord has impressed on me or shown me with my own family. My advice here is only the basics. A good start, perhaps, but not enough to reach the goals God has for you and your children. Ask Him to help you complete the task of teaching your children about Jesus.

We can be comforted knowing that some great men of God also understood they could not "get it right" without God's help. King David wrote to God saying, "Show me the way I should go, . . . lead me on level ground" (Psalm 143:8, 10 NIV). In the same way, you need to ask God to show you what He wants you to teach your children.

King Solomon wrote, "Trust in the LORD with all thine heart; . . . and he shall direct thy paths"

(Proverbs 3:5–6 KJV). Solomon was a very wise man. Like him, after God directs you regarding what to tell your children about Him, trust God and do what He shows you. Only then can you be confident you are telling your children what God wants them to know.

CHAPTER THREE

When Will You Tell Your Children About Jesus?

After reading the preceding chapter, the answer to that question should be obvious: *always!* We have already discussed that children learn the most from what you do rather than from what you say. Since they can and will watch what you do—whether it includes Jesus or not—every minute of every day, you are always teaching them. Even as you read this book they are learning something. What they learn depends on whether or not you tell them what you are reading about. Won't their mind-set be different if you tell them you are reading to learn better ways to teach them about Jesus, instead of their only knowing you are off reading some old book!

Naturally, there are many individual lessons about Jesus that you will have to teach in more detail for your children to really get to know and understand Jesus. The list of events from Jesus' life in chapter two includes good examples of such lessons. There is a logical order to these lessons. Your children's ages and what they can comprehend at various levels of maturity will impact your "lesson plans." So you have some planning to do. In this chapter we will learn when to put your plans in motion. However, no matter what your particular plan is, it is important that you get started—the sooner the better!

Dr. John Trent and others have recently published a book called *Parents' Guide to the Spiritual Growth of Children* (Tyndale House Publishers, 2000). This is an excellent and thorough resource for training your children as Christians. In the introduction to the chapter on teaching children about Jesus, they summarize the dilemma:

> *When you look at all your children need to learn—the Bible, who God is, what He's like and has done, how to have a personal relationship with Him, and what all of that means for their lives—it can seem as if you're standing behind a fully loaded dump truck as the driver raises the back. Out fall doctrine, parables, wisdom, history, truths, prophecy, miracles, guidelines for conduct, God's kingdom, faith, belief, sin and its consequences, laws, discipline, character development, and more— 4,000-plus years of revelation about God, God's dealings with humanity, Christian experience, and doctrinal development! And you have to pass all this on to your children in creative ways that take into account your family's uniqueness?*

Wow! I guess you'd better get started right away or you will NEVER GET IT DONE!

Please, don't think that way. Too many parents want to put off this task indefinitely thinking it will be *too* hard to teach *so much* about Jesus. Oh, I pray they would consider the price their children will pay for their inaction.

Remember: You have a lot of teaching time in front of you. You will need to consider the ability of each of your children to comprehend Christian concepts, and then get started with a plan. Most effective would be a plan that allows you to teach thousands of small, *living* lessons on a day-by-day basis. (Dumping a ton of facts on them in prolonged teaching sessions will probably not have the effect you planned.)

Before we discuss children at different ages and what they can understand, let's once again emphasize that parents are *always* teaching. Many lessons are understandable to children of all ages. Living lessons that show how we manage anger, whether or not we are truthful even when it hurts, and whether or not we love our neighbors are ones that even small children can learn by observation. Therefore, regardless of any intellectual teaching you may want to convey verbally to your children, never forget that the backdrop of your life *and your actions* are what they are watching every day. Be consistent and don't allow one of your living lessons to negate what you say. Live out what you want to teach.

Now, on to your children . . .

Infancy

If your child is yet to be born or was just recently born, what a blessed time this can be to begin his or her journey with Jesus. During these early months, which will pass too quickly, pray regularly with your child. God knows your child even in the womb (see Jeremiah 1:5), so get busy growing this relationship. Pray for your child's growth and health, and for a growing knowledge of Jesus in this young life.

Of course, you should add whatever other petitions you have for God about your child. Even before your child is born—or as soon as you are able to pray this prayer and mean it from the deepest part of your heart—I encourage you to give your child

> Before I formed thee in the belly I knew thee; and before thou camest forth out of the womb I sancti-fied thee . . .
> Jeremiah 1:5, KJV

back to God and place him or her in God's care.

A child is an incredible gift from God that comes with such great joy. We would be wrong and selfish to imagine that we either deserve or have the wisdom to manage such a great gift alone. For that reason, give your child back to God with an earnest request that He—and not you—be the one to make the plans and arrangements for this child's life. This is a difficult prayer to pray because we don't naturally want to give up control of such wonderful present. However, giving control to God is one of the most important lessons you will ever teach your children.

Toddler years

By the age of one or two, most children will be learning rapidly. The amount of words they know grows daily, and they will learn endless new skills and tricks with their newfound mobility. Part of their new vocabulary should be the name of Jesus. In fact I encourage you to use the names of God, Jesus and the Holy Spirit around your child so they become a part of his or her ever-expanding vocabulary. Don't be shy about introducing your child·to God!

This is the time to introduce the simple, eternal concepts of God. Tell your child that God is good, that God is love, and that Jesus loves them. This is also the time to model for your child that church attendance is a very high priority in a Christian's life. Let your son or daughter begin to experience the joy of celebrating Jesus with others. (Church is also the best place for Christian parents to meet other Christian parents and share the rewards and challenges of rearing Christian children.)

Preschool years

These are wonderful social and interactive years. What a great time to teach your children how to have a personal relationship with Jesus. During these years, tell them about praying and teach them to pray. Memorized prayers are a good way to pass along your heritage. I urge you, however, not to stop there. Ask your children for input regarding what to pray about. Pray from your heart and include petitions related to current happenings in your family's life. In the process show them how to pray and what to say to Jesus.

This age is also great for teaching children about sin. They are very much into learning what's right and what's wrong, and they are not afraid to tell you. The Hebrew word for "sin" has in its meaning the idea of "missing the mark," similar to the way that an arrow that doesn't hit a target misses the mark. Jesus has a plan for us and He has instructed us how to live. Not following His plan, missing the mark, is sin.

This is the time to tell them that sinning is wrong and that God punishes sin. Thankfully, Jesus took our punishment for us and we are forgiven.

At this age tell your children about what God does: He set the rules; He punishes sin; and yet He forgives us. For this we should always be thankful, and we can tell Him that in our prayers.

Elementary school age

When your children go off to school and experience life on their own, with no mom or dad to make decisions for them, their ability to cling to right instead of wrong will be put to the test. What can we tell them about Jesus now? Jesus was also tempted to do wrong. Yet He resisted,

Then Jesus was led by the Spirit into the desert to be tempted by the devil. After fasting forty days and forty nights, he was hungry. The tempter came to him and said, "If you are the Son of God, tell these stones to become bread." Jesus answered, "It is written: 'Man does not live on bread alone, but on every word that comes from the mouth of God.'" Then the devil took him to the holy city and had him stand on the highest point of the temple. "If you are the Son of God," he said, "throw yourself down. For it is written: 'He will command his angels concerning you, and they will lift you up in their hands, so that you will not strike your foot against a stone.'" Jesus answered him, "It is also written: 'Do not put the Lord your God to the test.'" Again, the devil took him to a very high mountain and showed him all the kingdoms of the world and their splendor. "All this I will give you," he said, "if you will bow down and worship me." Jesus said to him, "Away from me, Satan! For it is written: 'Worship the Lord your God, and serve him only.'" Then the devil left him, and angels came and attended him.

Matthew 4:1–11, NIV

and He resisted by clinging to the Word of God. (See Matthew 4:1–11.)

This is such a great time to tell your children how God's Word, the Bible, has instructions for our everyday living today. Take the opportunity to remind your child of Bible verses that apply to a dilemma your child is facing or will face. Tell him or her about Jesus, using Jesus' own words. What a beautiful way to grow the relationship between your child and God.

These years require the development of godly attributes as well. Teach and encourage patience, loyalty and love for others. Take the events of your child's life, use God's words to relate to those events, and your child will learn so much about Jesus.

Preteen and teen years

These are certainly critical years to need self-control, righteousness and joy! And adolescents can have all these things when they know Jesus. In these pivotal years, more than any other, what you do will teach your children what you believe. When parents are inconsistent—saying one thing and doing another—their credibility as teachers shrinks.

For example, how can a father effectively convince his thirteen-year-old son not to smoke if the father himself is a smoker? Likewise, teaching about Jesus will be difficult if your children do not see Jesus in you. When they observe you, do they see self-control? How about righteousness? What about joy? Do they see a peace that is attractive and desirable, or do they see conflict and unrest? Does the way you live lead them to Jesus, or chase them away?

What kinds of things should you say to your adolescent children? This is a great time to share your knowledge and relationship with Jesus with your children. Tell them how you came to know Jesus, how you deal with temptation around you, and what ways you have found to maintain your walk with the Lord. Perhaps you can share Bible verses that are particularly meaningful to you and give examples of how you use them to direct your actions. Tell your teens and preteens about the special people who have impacted your life decisions. Relate how that has kept you closer to Jesus.

I encourage you to not let a day go by without your growing children praying with you. They need to hear you say the name of Jesus in prayer and see you reading your Bible. That is how you really tell them that Jesus is real. Remember, your actions speak louder than your words. Your children are watching you to see if your actions and words give the same message.

Special times

There are many special, emotionally charged, times in a child's life that create fertile teaching environments. Take advantage of these times. They are windows of opportunity to speak God's truths into your child's soul.

When a friend has hurt your child, remind him or her of why we must forgive others. (See Matthew 6:14–15.) When you or your child is mourning the death of a friend

> For if ye forgive men their trespasses, your heavenly Father will also forgive you: But if ye forgive not men their trespasses, neither will your Father forgive your trespasses.
>
> Matthew 6:14–15, KJV

or family member, speak of how God is always present and of the joy of finally being with Jesus. (See First Thessalonians 4:16–18.) When your children are frustrated, impatient or angry about situations in today's world, remind them of Jesus' glorious return. (See Revelation 19:11–16.) When your children are in need of comfort, refer them to the Bible and to prayer.

For the Lord himself shall descend from heaven with a shout, with the voice of the archangel, and with the trump of God: and the dead in Christ shall rise first: Then we which are alive and remain shall be caught up together with them in the clouds, to meet the Lord in the air: and so shall we ever be with the Lord. Wherefore comfort one another with these words.

1 Thessalonians 4:16–18, KJV

And I saw heaven opened, and behold a white horse; and he that sat upon him was called Faithful and True, and in righteousness he doth judge and make war. His eyes were as a flame of fire, and on his head were many crowns; and he had a name written, that no man knew, but he himself. And he was clothed with a vesture dipped in blood: and his name is called The Word of God. And the armies which were in heaven followed him upon white horses, clothed in fine linen, white and clean. And out of his mouth goeth a sharp sword, that with it he should smite the nations: and he shall rule them with a rod of iron: and he treadeth the winepress of the fierceness and wrath of Almighty God. And he hath on his vesture and on his thigh a name written, KING OF KINGS, AND LORD OF LORDS.

Revelation 19:11–16, KJV

CHAPTER FOUR ⑤

How Will You Tell Your Children About Jesus?

The earlier chapters of this book have already given you ideas about *how* to tell your children about Jesus. Pardon me if I got ahead of myself, but it was important to talk a little bit about the *how* even as we talked about the *what* and the *when* of telling your children about Jesus.

In this chapter I will stick only to the *how*. I mention again, however, that this is a brief book written simply to motivate parents. More thorough works about how to teach and raise

Christian children are out there. In the previous chapter I mentioned *Parents' Guide to the Spiritual Growth of Children*. A second outstanding reference is *Faithful Parents, Faithful Kids* by Greg Johnson and Mike Yorkey (Tyndale House Publishers, 1993). This second book is truly a "how to" manual for parents that gives sound advice. While I hope that my little book gets parents excited about raising Christian children, I count on you parents to find more in-depth guidance from your church's pastoral staff, as well as in more comprehensive works written for that purpose.

How you tell your children about Jesus will be determined by what you want to accomplish in this critical task of parenthood. The prize of Christianity is eternal life with Jesus, our Lord. Your children will reach that end by acquiring a personal, loving relationship with God. Through your work as a parent, that relationship can become a reality.

Your teaching of truths about God, your demonstration of the reality of God through your worship, and your trust in the truth of His Word are the foundations for your children's relationship with their Savior. You, as the parent, play a pivotal role in successfully establishing that relationship. You are the key that determines the likelihood of your children's salvation. *How* you fulfill that role can greatly enhance the likelihood of your success.

In *Faithful Parents, Faithful Kids*, Greg Johnson wrote,

> It's our relationship with our kids that matters most to God, not their good behavior or whether we escorted them through the church doors every time they were open.

Isn't that interesting? To prepare your children for their eternal relationship with God, you first train them in an earthly relationship with you. Here are a couple of good ways to nurture this relationship (part of the *how* of telling your child about Jesus):

Always take a kid along on jaunts to the grocery store or pharmacy. As you watch the road and they read road signs, it is a good time to ask questions about their lives, getting to know them better and growing their relationship with you. Also, fun family nights with some "traditions" that they will remember are wonderful for building your relationships and your heritage. At our house, an evening of Monopoly® has often filled this role.

Don't get me wrong now; you are no substitute for God! Yet you *are* your children's teacher. From you they will learn what to expect in their parent-child relationship with God. If you do it right, they will learn the truth about how God relates to us as a father (parent). You are their model. When you show truthfulness, faithfulness and goodness, your children will be better able to understand those attributes in God. Conversely, if you prove to be erratic, inconsistent and untrustworthy in your relationship with them, your children will have difficulty coming into a relationship with a God who is more loving than what they know now.

So how important is the *how*? CRITICAL! Your children have a free will. What they choose in life depends on what they learn and what they love. You are in charge of both of these areas. Your daily living *is* their classroom. (How perfect to realize that the Bible is written to guide us in this very same setting.) Your children will learn what you show them. Have fun telling them! Whether or not they love what you teach them depends on your *how* in teaching them.

Greg Johnson (*Faithful Parents, Faithful Kids*) compiled a list of responses from children who were asked, "What were the top things your parents did to point you to Christ?" The top answers included:

⑨ "They never shoved their faith down my throat. They read the Bible to me and were living examples of being a Christian."

⑨ "I saw their consistent relationship with God."

⑨ "They read their Bibles in front of me."

⑨ "My parents never bad-mouthed the church in front of me."

⑨ "They encouraged us to have a daily quiet time."

⑨ "Mom explained the gospel at an early age."

⑨ "They instilled in us a love for Jesus, the church, and Christian music. They also taught us to have a love for the truth."

§ "As soon as I was old enough to understand, they showed me that their relationship with God was not enough for me to
gain salvation."

These are just a few of the many *how* issues
to consider. There is so much more you can do.

Live out your values and let your children
be wide-eyed observers. Live out your relationship with God where your children can see it.
This is no time to be silent. Tell your children
your thoughts and tell them about God's con-
stant impact on your life. Have fun doing it!
These lessons are joyous. Never think of them
as work.

Have books about God in your home all the
time. (Don't have them just sitting on the table.
Read them and share them with your children.)
Place funny and thoughtful signs about God on
your doors and walls. Fill your house with God.
Put a bold bumper sticker on that says in some
way that you love Jesus. Be a Sunday school

teacher. (It's really not hard—I do it!) Volunteer as a family for service duties like cleaning the church or serving at the soup kitchen. Listen to only Christian music in your home and watch Christian videos with your children, too.

The power of music and drama, for good or for evil, is very great. Take a serious stand against worldly music and movies in your home. No parent is powerful enough to overcome these media. They will teach more evil than you can teach good, and the words and images they implant in your child can last a lifetime. This is a most important *how*.

Promoting positive peer groups with your children is another important role for parents. Children will adopt the values of their peer group when they realize that this is how you get along and become accepted. If the peer group runs contrary to the values you teach, you will have a tough battle (and one confused child) on your hands. Look instead for groups that emphasize and reinforce the values you have already taught your child. The church youth group is a good place to start, but you can find many other organizations that suit these criteria and that your children can enjoy.

Weeding out bad influences in your child's life is also your job. I often remind parents of this in our office visits, especially in the early teen years when friendships are developing. One of my favorite sayings goes like this:

> You cannot tell your children who their friends are going to be. Forcing this never works. However, you *can* tell your children who their friends are *not* going to be.

This is one way of directing them away from bad influences and towards positive influences.

Some other special areas of importance that I ask every parent to consider are cursing, smoking, drinking and attitudes about sex. How you manage these behaviors yourself and in other people all are important parts of *how* you teach your children about Jesus. Your children probably already know a lot of what is wrong and right in these areas. *How* will you demonstrate your values to them in the classroom of your life?

I would like to mention a few more pointers in this area of *how* to tell your children about Jesus. These are ideas I've picked up from friends, pastors, books, the teachings of others, and my own family. I hope you can find a use for them with your children as I have with mine.

Always begin your meals with prayer.

This is not rocket science. The Bible directs us to do so.

Say an evening prayer with your children as they lie down to sleep.

There is something very special about this time of each day. Children are more receptive. The setting is more intimate. I encourage you to model praying on your knees at their bed. It is good for them to see you on your knees before God.

Pray before traveling.

Demonstrate your trust in God's protection over your family during these times.

Ask your children what they have learned about God.

After church, Sunday school or any other significant event, review what truth about God was evident at that event or in that sermon or lesson.

Have regular devotional time.

Make it a regular activity to spend time daily with God, both as an individual and as a family. These times can include prayer, reading or just quiet meditation. Let your children choose the method at times. But no matter what, give God the time.

Attend church regularly.
Here you will all learn more and more about God. Worshiping with a group is wonderful reinforcement for your daily worship. Making Christian friends will increase your confidence in following the Lord. Surrounding yourself with Christian friends will provide models of Christian behavior for you and your children. Simply going to church will not, however, get you or your children into heaven. That feat is accomplished only through a relationship with Jesus Christ—something they should be learning about at home.

Use Bibles and devotions that your children can understand.
Worshiping God is fun. Language or references that are too difficult or too dry will turn chil-

dren off. Find Bibles and stories and videos that your children can understand and enjoy.

Create a Christian heritage for your children and ask God to direct your steps every day.

To round out this list of how to tell your children about Jesus let me also give you a few things that you should *not* do:

Don't push your children.
Rather, lead them. Show an interest in what they do and how much they understand. That way you can discuss truths about God in a way that they can grasp.

Don't resist change.
Remember that you're human. You can also be taught and led. Can you take some steps toward

them so that they feel better taking steps toward you?

Don't compromise on biblical principles. Be human and teachable, but know where God's directions are clear and never stray from them.

Don't allow pornography or worldly magazines (*Teen, Cosmopolitan,* etc.) in your home. The impact of the images in those kinds of magazines is powerful on your children's minds. It will be very difficult to overcome this evil if it is allowed to take root.

Don't "fellowship" with the television on. As interesting and as fun as you may be, the attraction to those moving, colorful images will win your audience. Your words will fall on deafened (or at least preoccupied) ears.

Most important of all, **don't ever give up!**
(See Philippians 3:12–14.)

> . . . I press on to take hold of that for which
> Christ Jesus took hold of me. Brothers, I
> do not consider myself yet to have taken
> hold of it. But one thing I do: Forgetting
> what is behind and straining toward what
> is ahead, I press on toward the goal to win
> the prize for which God has called me
> heavenward in Christ Jesus.
>
> Philippians 3:12–14, NIV

Then What Do You Do?

Smile. Be encouraged. Enjoy that you've come to the end of this book!

Well, perhaps I don't want you to be too joyous about that. I do pray, however, that you find joy in your relationship with Jesus Christ and in the experience of teaching your children about Him. There is no greater joy as a parent than to know that your children walk with God. (See Third John 4.)

Sadly, as a pediatrician I know many parents whose children have died. However, those parents who

> I have no greater joy than to hear that my children are walking in the truth.
>
> 3 John 4, NIV

know—I mean *really know*—that their children are in heaven have a joy that is greater that even this great sorrow. That is the joy I want for you and for all parents. I want you to know beyond the shadow of a doubt that your children have an eternity with Jesus.

So what must you do now? It's time to begin telling them. Tell them about Jesus. It is your job; the job does not belong either to the school or to Sunday school teachers. You are their teacher and you are their best teacher. No one can do this job as well—or as badly—as you can.

Remember, you will tell your children about Jesus in one way or another no matter what you do. You can teach indifference or you can teach a relationship that leads to eternal life. You can choose to teach either lesson, but you cannot choose not to choose. Your children learn from you all the time. Your children are learning from you even now. What are you teaching?

Reading about Jesus and His disciples always reminds me of parenting. His followers were indeed children in their understanding of God's kingdom. They had learned wrongly because no one had taught them the true message. Jesus did not neglect His role. In fact, He taught them so well that they keenly taught others who taught others, who taught others. And we are still the beneficiaries of their faithful belief and teaching!

You, too, have disciples. You are their rabbi, their teacher. You, too, can impact generation after generation if you tell your children about Jesus. Tell them with a love and a passion that makes them want to repeat this process with their children. You can have—and pass on—this heritage.

As Jesus left the earth for the last time, He gave dramatic instructions to His followers. He said:

> Therefore go and make disciples of all nations, . . . teaching them to obey everything I have commanded you. And surely I am with you always, to the very end of the age. (Matthew 28:19–20 NIV)

You have been given a nation, a people—*your family*. No one said that your nation was going to be a large one! Go, therefore, and make disciples, knowing that Jesus is with you. *Go*, and tell your children about Jesus.

ABOUT THE   AUTHOR

Alan Getts, M.D. is a Christian pediatrician in Augusta, Georgia. Dr. Getts graduated from the U.S. Military Academy at West Point, New York, and from the College of Medicine at the University of Illinois. At West Point he graduated as a "Distinguished Cadet" in the top five percent of his class, and at the University of Illinois he was named a James Scholar in Independent Study.

After twenty years of medicine in the Army uniform, Dr. Getts entered the private practice of pediatrics in Augusta where he practices today. He is blessed with three children and a lovely wife who all love the Lord. They worship together at In Focus Ministry Center in Evans, Georgia.

As Dr. Getts' first book, *Who Will Tell Your Children About Jesus?* was birthed to meet the clear need he sees for his patients and their families to know Jesus more. Pediatricians endure many sorrows with their patients' families— none so sad, however, as those with families who do not know the Lord. Dr. Getts places this book in the hand of each parent at their child's first birthday to encourage them to begin telling their children about Jesus.

Recommended Resources for Further Study §

As You Walk Along the Way—How to Lead Your Child on the Path of Spiritual Discipline. Carla R. Williams. Horizon Books. Camp Hill, PA. 2001. The principles and disciplines included in this interactive, how-to manual address a child's physical, emotional, mental, and spiritual growth from birth through the teenage years. It gives parents ideas for laying a spiritual foundation of practicing spiritual disciplines of prayer, confession, fasting, worship, service, study, celebration, solitude, and guidance. Available for purchase at your local Christian bookstore or online at www.amazon.com and www.christianpublications.com.

Focus on the Family Complete Book of Baby and Child Care. Paul C. Reisser, MD et. al. Tyndale House Publishers, Inc. Wheaton, IL. 1997. Available for purchase your local Christian bookstore or online at www.amazon.com.

Faithful Parents, Faithful Kids. Greg Johnson and Mike Yorkey. Tyndale House Publishers, Inc. Wheaton, IL. 1993. (See pages 68, 69) This book is out of print, but used copies are available for purchase on line at www.amazon.com.

Parents' Guide to the Spiritual Growth of Children (Heritage Builders). Dr. John Trent (Editor), et.al. Tyndale House Publishers, Inc. Wheaton, IL. 2000. (See pages 52, 53) Available for purchase at your local Christian bookstore or online at www.amazon.com.

To order additional copies of

Who Will
Tell Your
Children
About
Jesus?

Have your credit card ready and call

Toll free: (877) 421-READ (7323)

or send $11.95* each plus $3.95 S&H**

to
WinePress Publishing
PO Box 428
Enumclaw, WA 98022

*Washington residents please add 8.4% tax.
**Add $1.00 S&H for each additional book ordered.